I0528426

FIRE FROM THE HEART
2024

WINNERS OF THE
MURIEL'S JOURNEY POETRY PRIZE

THREE OCEAN PRESS

All poems and text © 2024 by their respective authors.
Design © 2024 Three Ocean Press.

All rights reserved. No part of this publication may be reproduced, stored in a retrieval system, or transmitted, in any form or by any means, electronic, mechanical, photocopying, recording, or otherwise, without prior written permission of the publisher.

All characters in this book are fictional. Any resemblance to persons living or dead is purely coincidental.

Library and Archives Canada Cataloguing in Publication

Title: Fire from the heart, 2024 : winners of the 2024 Muriel's Journey Poetry Prize.
Other titles: Winners of the 2024 Muriel's Journey Poetry Prize
Identifiers: Canadiana 20240525647 | ISBN 9781988915531 (softcover)
Subjects: CSH: Canadian poetry (English)—21st century. | LCGFT: Poetry.
Classification: LCC PS8293.1 .F579 2024 | DDC C811/.6080971—dc23

Editor: Kyle Hawke
Cover and Book Designer: Kyle Hawke
Front and back cover art: ©2024 James Picard

Three Ocean Press
Vancouver, BC
778.321.0636
info@threeoceanpress.com
www.threeoceanpress.com

First publication, November 2024

Muriel's Journey

Year 6 of the Muriel's Journey Poetry Prize! This time around, I'd like to give a shoutout to all the people who didn't make the final cut. Every poem matters! While both our judges and first readers are highly experienced poets, their ultimate selection depends on many, often unpredictable factors. So — a big thank you and hooray to all the poets across Canada who sent us their beautiful heart- and mindfelt work. You are seen, you are read, you are appreciated.

Kyle Hawke continues to be my anchor in this. I am so grateful for his sensitivities as an editor, publisher, and all-round brilliant mind. Many thanks go to our judges, Candie Tanaka, Susan Cormier, and George Honesty, Jr. Read their statement! The fiery cover art is by James Picard. Thanks to our first readers, Sally Quon and Natasha Rose Sanders-Kay, and to Tova Mori, our indefatigable administrative assistant. A big shoutout, too, to Heart of the City and Word Vancouver, who continue to support us by inviting us to their events.

ISABELLA MORI, on the traditional, ancestral and unceded territory of the Sḵwx̱wú7mesh (Squamish), Səlílwətaʔ/Selilwitulh (Tsleil-Waututh) and xʷməθkʷəy̓əm (Musqueam) Nations (Vancouver, BC, Canada)

About Muriel and the Prize

Muriel was a social justice activist, poet, and spoken word artist of Indigenous heritage from the Gitxsan nation's Owl Clan who spent a lot of time in the Downtown Eastside. In her work, she always explored new ways of expressing herself, always talked and wrote about what's urgent and important. Her energy was like fireworks and her hugs legendary.

Muriel died in November of 2018. At Muriel's memorial at the DTES' Listening Post, someone related that on her last day, Muriel said that while she was leaving, she was still continuing her journey. The text was accompanied by a picture of the sunrise on the day she died. Isabella was moved by this to do her part in Muriel's continued journey and decided to start a poetry prize in Muriel's honour.

Everyone liked Muriel. She encouraged creative people of all stripes to continue on their path of creativity and social justice. With the Muriel's Journey Poetry Prize, we hope to pass on inspiration and strength to all who create with a sense of justice in mind.

Because Muriel always did things a little differently, we're doing this poetry prize a little differently, too. Being keenly aware of how subjective the judging of poetry can be, we give a prize to a poet randomly selected from the longlist of those who met the entry requirement of "lively, outspoken ideas … speak your mind and let the world know what you think … look at your subject in an unexpected way … take a risk in your composition … be frank and unreserved." Another change is our 'entry fee', which consists of people showing how they contribute to their community. Lastly, we have two first prizes, a general one and one specifically for a poet with close ties to the Downtown Eastside.

All poems in this collection were submitted and subsequently were selected by judges as the winners of the sixth annual Muriel's Journey Poetry Prize.

Prizes were awarded at an online ceremony on September 22, 2024 as part of the Word Vancouver literary arts festival. The ceremony was hosted from the traditional and unceded territory of the Musqueam, Squamish, and Tsleil-Waututh peoples, but included winners reading from their home territories, as noted in their Community Involvement statements at the end of this book.

ORGANIZERS
Isabella Mori
Kyle Hawke

JUDGES
Susan Cormier
George Honesty, Jr.
Candie Tanaka

Special thanks to the Vancouver Public Library, the Carnegie Centre, and the Heart of the City Festival for allowing us a platform to build on, as well as to Glenn Mori, who worked out the slushing system for the poems. Thanks also to Cecily Nicholson, Diane Wood, and past organizer Rudolf Penner, without whom this whole project would have never happened.

The Muriel's Journey Poetry Prize honours the vitality, vivacity, and outspoken presence of poet-activist Muriel Marjorie, who passed on in the fall of 2018. As an Indigenous social justice activist, poet, and spoken word artist, what Muriel had to say would often literally wake you up. Her enthusiastic encouragement of innovative creative endeavours was infectious.

The Muriel's Journey Poetry Prize is open to all residents of Canada and to Canadians living abroad. No submission fee is charged; instead, those entering are asked to provide a statement of their community involvement to demonstrate their active effort to improve the world around them. First prize is $100. The DTES prize is also $100 and celebrates poets with a deep connection to Vancouver's Downtown Eastside. Second prize is $50. Fortuna's Choice rewards one randomly selected poem with $35. Judges look for lively, outspoken texts that present ideas in unexpected ways.

For information on the Muriel's Journey Poetry Prize, please contact the organizers at poetryprize@murielsjourney.com or visit their Facebook page.

www.murielsjourney.com

Contents

You
Richard-Yves Sitoski

Weekends find you on the couch
eating popsicles with authority
while I search for a job in a town
where they put buttons in collection plates.
Your photosynthetic hands rejoice
when exposed to nightlights
and when you nap you are an oven
cooling after baking bread.
The same things make us cry so that
shedding tears we are perfect rhymes.
You tolerate the neighbour whose face
is a shaking house when a door is slammed
and you hold me in a way that I don't
become a spruce tree crawling with
budworms. You make me happy enough
to face a future alone though I lack
your confidence with sunlight
as a sculpture medium. Believe me
when I say expect a jealous god to rise
from a vat of pesticides and come for us
with bureaucratic intent. But I will not
look back as he chases us Eurydice.
So grab the hem of my hospital gown.
I've got this. His carnivore's breath
in your hair is so last year. His lampblack
fingers will catch in the quantum field
we swim through. We shall thrive and sing
down clouds from a sky so blue it's ruthless
while he remains what he is. An emo kid
jealous of the living — we who are so smug
with our tiny sandwiches after a funeral.

GROUNDED

Phoenix Winter

I. Earth

II. Bare earth
   green, fallow
     Gardens — Cottonwood, Strathcona
   Big trees
     twisted roots

   My community
                 year after year
     Peace is carried
     Held high

III. Upheaval Earth.
       Bare Earth
         Earth

     I have honoured you
       Tall trees
         twisted with
             pruning
         surviving
           offering shade
         CUT
         CHOPPED
         HACKED

I cry out tears

     So hollow

IV. Concrete. Upheaval Earth. Bare Earth.   Earth.
   I remember I remember I remember
   the rustle of wet leaves in the rain
   I hear trees talking
      remember what we once were,
         what we were meant to be
   Never forget...

   V. Earth.

I Want to Sit on My Silence
Atma Frans

Dangle my legs
from its lips

Instead, I'm stuck
in its throat

scrambling up
the slippery slope

Fingers slip
on secrets and spit

Shame sweeps down
the tongue

clots
in my mouth

Lungs cough up
goldfish and snakes

I grab
the tail of my rage

Eileen Wiscombe
Painted Vistas

Where coniferous meets deciduous
a plethora of life erupts
Water veins entwine the landscape
While softly sculpting new vistas
A myriad of green streaks across the canvas
Sunset hues paint the sky
The cool smooth stone shields the earth
And I...
I am lost amongst the soft caress of blue
that gently lulls my soul into peace and calm
It's a wonder to behold
A sight that must be seen
For one can truly never comprehend
All these shades of green
But seven souls they knew
just how to frame these masterpieces
For in the land of the Algonquin
Nature's a painting come to life

Clockwork, morning, alarm
Phyllis Cherret

This morning I shuffle out of the bed's sweet
embrace in time to catch the poignant moment
when the bullet exits the skull, that vivid flourish
of scarlet intermixed with ivory, a spray in many
senses of the word, and on the screen another
beauty folds to the floor and the camera cuts away

I offer coffee, while on the screen they fling their
fists and fucks across the flattened
rooms, and I imagine how their knuckles bruise
and split on the recalcitrance of bone

and how you haven't looked away

> (and how they get up when the
> camera isn't watching, with the
> small wound and the big one
> still dripping, walk to their cars
> and stop once on the way home,
> buy bread and flowers for the table,
> walk their dogs and toss their pocket change
> into the saucer by the door)

and how you haven't looked away

THE OTHER
Diana Hayes

> The Other is dissimilar to and the opposite of
> the Self, of Us, and of the Same.
> —*The Oxford Companion to Philosophy*

One

Tell me when it began. An eternity recalls my childhood shadow.
The toddler-in-arms could not tell the difference between here and there,
   returning or wanting to stay.

Did anyone make a diagnosis? I lit up on the X-ray table and medical
   students swarmed.
Barium milkshakes, speculation by omission. My insides turned inside-out.

Where was your mother? They tore her from me, a reversal of birth. Her
   coat buttons went flying.
After that, blue lights from croup tent rooms formed a runway down the
   corridor. I wandered. I might well have left the building.

What else? Something followed me from behind the walls of that infirmary.
   It spoke in code,
whispered phrases. The repetition dogged me.

What else? Men of the cloth whispered the same phrases. Was I being
   called up or called down?
The voices rolled like the prodrome for thunder. Vertigo's dance, perpetual.

Two

What did you do next? I picked up stones and polished them. Scribbled
   verses in tiny journals.
I stayed awake and listened to crickets and owls. Fell shy of the shoreline
   and landed in the lake.

over

I remember that lake. It tempted me. I couldn't swim. Skated on it instead. Sharp blades,
breath like frost, shoot the duck in long succession. Run. Skate. Run.

Did the whisper-voice follow? Behind the brick walls of the Maritime house
before dawn. I woke to creaking sounds
on the stairs and lost my voice. A black robe brushing the hardwood floor.
A crone's shadow. Old, bereft, calling.

I bet you wanted to leave. My legs froze. The crone tied them in knots. This
time the bardo was quicksand.
I could not get up.

Tell me more. Her gaze broke and I woke. After that my mother placed a
blue light in my night room.

Three

Where are you now? I'm gulping oxygen like goldfish at the surface of the
pond.

What do you mean? I burned my doll's dress and made her a swimsuit to
wear. I named her *Betty Nose,*
she was my favourite doll. She had no reason to breathe. She was happy at
the bottom of the lake.

Did you change your name? Once. I penciled in Delphina, but the blank
stares of the teachers haunted me.

Did the cat get your tongue? I preferred growls, hollers, hissing. Feral. I kept
words locked up in my journal.
One night I spoke in tongues. Echoes came up from the ravine. I ran, skates
slung over my shoulder. I dreamed of that frozen lake.

Did you skate in pageants? I was a rabbit with full lop ears, a suit of white
fur, whiskers made from pipe cleaners.
Then I became the goddess of maize. Demeter on ice. Swaying in arena
rows.

I hate to ask. Did the voice return? Up from under the ice. After a hard rain.
    The glass dome of the lake
cracked and whined like the angry wind's whistle. I heard it say: *just this
    once, step out from your figure-eights.*

Four

*You're not going to believe this. The voice that always whispers turned up in
    my dream.* It slithers like a chorus in the middle of a song.
The moonflower feigns sleep after dark. Seahorse silhouettes glaze the
    folding petals. I know, I was there. It was Ulrike's wake.

Well now you've lost me, a segue or a maze? The poems shape-shift just like
    the corn goddess on skates. The voice appears
in lowercase, between lines. Shows up under the ice.

Are you still afraid? The portents are disguised but always tell the truth.
    Deep menace, ancient argument, a fatal wound.
That poem followed me home. How the rushing water washed my
    trepidation, made me forget the mountain.

You were bridging the white water. I was preparing for winter. Feeding fire
    from the earth. Far from the shadow's edge.
This was Haidée's song. Remember?

Run. Skate. Run. If only my ankles could carry me back across the lake.
    Centre of gravity fails. Don't grow old.
Tuck the arms in to save energy before the bell-lap sprint.

Five

Still sleep with a blue light? Yes.

Poet Hands
C.E. Hoffman

My mother's father wrote a poem called *Rig Hands*.
I never read it.
Never met him.
He was busy cooking on cruises/oil rigs,
boxing, racing,
dying at forty(ish.)

I try to imagine
what he wrote
(it got published!)
maybe an ode
to the working man
the ones who
sweat
fight
dance
drink 'til their bottle is empty,
'til their heart is dried up,
'til their family is afraid.

I cannot write a poem called *Rig Hands*.
My fists blush w/
virgin knuckles.
They cannot throw a punch
slam a shot
charm a girl into giving me
her future.

My skin is soft.
My wrists are thin.
My reach is so far
and my grasp
so small.

On the Front Lines at the Court of Death
Jessica Lee McMillan

When my heart is weighed of what it witnesses, it will be feather
light for all the wrong reasons. It will be squeezed of all its
muscle. The courthouse "guest list" tallies poverty crimes from
the revolving door of welfare and jail. The reference weight does
not understand a crater-faced parent—black moon eyes—rolling
their infant through metal detector gates past the sheriff and into
the waiting room of finger-smeared brochures in legalese, labelled
plain English curling over plexiglass stands—all spoils of purgatory
on paper—lifetimes of dockets and transcripts and on the desks
newspapers spin NIMBY obituaries, leaving out those who failed
to live. Necropolitics is the scale of life weighed in sponsored ink.
Admission to heaven's gate is rigged for kings and sycophants.
No Judge can weigh a heart pulled from the deepest pit of the
living. When my heart is weighed of what it witnesses, it will be
feather light. Squeezed of its muscle, like a fist of air from where I
will blow a kiss for all those squeezed out of existence.

FIRST PRIZE
Richard-Yves Sitoski

I am a songwriter, performance poet and the 2019–2023 Poet Laureate of Owen Sound, Ontario, on the territory of the Saugeen Ojibway Nation. Works in *Arc*, *Prairie Fire*, *Train*, and *The Fiddlehead*. As laureate, my duties came with a mandate to explore ecological issues in my community, and included environmental art interventions and site-specific social justice projects centring on homelessness. I am co-editor, with Penn Kemp, of *Poems in Response to Peril: An Anthology in Support of Ukraine*, profits from which went to displaced Ukrainian cultural workers.

SECOND PRIZE
Atma Frans

Atma Frans' poetry won first prize in *Quagmire Magazine*'s Poetry Contest, and was a finalist in contests run by *Freefall Magazine*, Oxford Brookes University, *The Malahat Review*, *CV2*, and *Sunspot Literary Journal*. Her poetry was nominated for the National Magazine Award and has been published widely in literary magazines. In her writing, Atma searches for the voice beneath her personas: woman, mother, trauma survivor, designer, queer, author. She lives on the unceded territory of the Sḵwx̱wú7mesh people in Gibsons, B.C. where she hikes, swims, and facilitates a writing group for the Federation of B.C Writers and participates in memoir collective.

Muriel's Journey Poetry Prize 2024 Winners
Community Involvement

Downtown Eastside Prize
Phoenix Winter

I am grateful to live on the territory of the Squamish, Musqueam, and Tsleil-Waututh people. I am a founding member of the DTES Writers Collective and the DTES Writers Festival. I led the FireWriters for over ten years at Carnegie and the group is now called Discovery Writers and is led by one of our members.

As a patron of the Carnegie, I was on the Board of the Centre for eleven years and president for five of those.

One of my biggest accomplishments is being a mother.

Fortuna's Choice
Eileen Wiscombe

Living in the suburbs of the GTA in Ontario, Canada, where I myself grew up, as well as raised my kids, I join in on local community clean-up projects to participate in keeping our community clean and safe. My creative spark was thankfully reignited a few years back... this time through words, poetry & prose, for which I am truly grateful. It came at a time where it allowed me to heal, learn, grow, and give me back my spark... my passion. I write what I feel, or where my mind takes me... it's a rollercoaster of a ride.

HONOURABLE MENTION
Phyllis Cherret

I am an unsettled settler poet living in Treaty 1 territory. I belong to the local Writer's Guild and volunteer critiquing poetry in that community, and occasionally packing surplus medical supplies for distribution to various countries in need (limited participation right now as I have Long Covid).

HONOURABLE MENTION
Diana Hayes

Diana Hayes was born in Toronto and has lived on the east and west coasts of Canada. She received her B.A. and M.F.A. in Creative Writing (UVic and UBC) and has seven published poetry books, most recently *Sapphire and the Hollow Bone* by Ekstasis Editions (2023). She launched Raven Chapbooks in 2019, an indie press for small edition poetry chapbooks. Previously, she worked as program director for Theatre Alive literary readings on Salt Spring for three decades. She has lived on Salt Spring Island—the traditional and unceded territory of the Hul'q'umi'num' and SENĆOŦEN speaking peoples—since 1981.

HONOURABLE MENTION
C.E. Hoffman

C.E. Hoffman is a Canadian author, poet, publisher, and screenwriter living on Treaty 6 Territory. They edit *Punk Monk Magazine* (2012–present), elevating femme/queer/ alt writers in the local and global community, and do the same on their podcast *Scribbles and Spills*. They have hosted/organized several spoken word events, including Speak Your Peace, which creates a safe space for first-time participants. Find their books (and more) at cehoffman. net and follow them on Twitter @CEHoffman2.

HONOURABLE MENTION
Jessica Lee McMillan

I am grateful to write and live on the unceded and unsurrendered land known as New Westminster, British Columbia of the Halkomelem-speaking Peoples.

I contribute to my community through the non-profit work I have been doing for nearly fifteen years, including teaching at-risk youth, new Canadians and refugees and assisting people with multiple barriers for over a decade in getting access to justice through my frontline work at Legal Aid. When I worked downtown, I regularly worked at the courthouse in the DTES and found new ways every day to bring some humanity into the process of getting legal counsel for vulnerable people who often felt frustrated with the bureaucracy. I committed to learning about community partners and finding ways to provide support.

Judges' Statement

Selecting the runners-up for this contest was quite challenging, given the level of quality and talent of the entries. Each of the judges had unique ideas on what constitutes a prize-worthy poem, and it took us an entire month of debating and discussing — each of us championing our favorite pieces and passionately expounding upon its merits — until we were able to settle on a final selection we could all agree upon.

One poem, however, we all immediately agreed upon and needed no further discussion: our winner, the simply-titled "You." With its mélange of rapid-fire metaphors and snapshot moments, this poem is an hors d'oeuvre tray of intriguing, delightful references and inferences that hint of a complex relationship beyond description. Its tone is both cheekily dark and whimsically uplifting — a triumph of words.

SUSAN CORMIER was the 2022 winner of the CBC Prize in Non-Fiction, and has won or been shortlisted for such awards as CBC's Prize in Poetry, *Arc Magazine*'s Poem of the Year, Anvil Press/*SubTerrain Magazine*'s Lush Triumphant, and the Federation of B.C. Writers' Literary Writes. She is the producer of the Vancouver Story Slam live storytelling competition. Her nonfiction book, *Dead Bees Still Sting*, is forthcoming from Greystone Books in 2026.

GEORGE HONESTY, JR. has been a line cook, a wheelchair ramp installer, a malt shop soda jerk employee of the month, and a mechanic on World War II go-carts. All the while, George scribbled verses and hummed melodies for treble clef notation. He resides in a shack in Surrey with his dog Spot and his cat Moo-Moo.

CANDIE TANAKA is a multiracial trans writer, artist, librarian, and graduate of The Writer's Studio program at Simon Fraser University. Their first YA book, *Baby Drag Queen*, was published with Orca Books in April 2023. They've also published work in *Resonance: Essays on the Craft of Life and Writing* with Anvil Press and *This Will Only Take A Minute: Canadian Flash Fiction* with Guernica Editions. Learn more at candietanaka.com.

www.ingramcontent.com/pod-product-compliance
Lightning Source LLC
Chambersburg PA
CBHW070958120626
46546CB00004B/1675